1770-1827

ℬEETHOVEN

1770-1827

$\mathscr{B}$EETHOVEN

TODTRI

© 1995 Bookman International bv
Houtweg 11, 1251 CR Laren (NH)
The Netherlands

For this present English language edition: Todtri Productions, Ltd.,
New York

Text: Jeroen Koolbergen
Translation: Van Splunteren/Burret
Lay-out: ADM, Pieter van Delft

This edition published in 1996 by Todtri Productions Limited P.O.
Box 572, New York, NY 10116-0572   FAX: (212) 279-1241

Printed and bound in Italy

ISBN 1-880908-80-8

Introduction

In 1770, the year in which Ludwig van Beethoven was born, Wolgang Amadeus Mozart was fourteen years old and astonishing the world with his musical maturity. Franz Joseph Haydn, in contrast, was already forty–eight. Living at the castle of the Esterházys, where he conducted the Count's private orchestra and where, constantly obliged to produce new compositions for the court concerts, he felt almost a prisoner. Mozart died in 1791, perhaps having briefly met Beethoven, but Haydn lived until 1809. For a while, the latter was the teacher of the young Beethoven who, in 1792, had also settled in Vienna. Although Haydn and Beethoven did not get on particularly well, Haydn was a fair enough man to openly recognize the genius in Beethoven's early compositions.

Mozart and Haydn had determined musical life in Vienna, but within ten years of Beethoven establishing himself there, he was regarded as the natural successor of these two great musicians and played an eccentric leading role in Viennese musical life. In those ten years Beethoven succeeded in transforming the music of the Classic period into music of a complexity and depth heard never before – and in a new style which was completely his own.

Few of Beethoven's contempories understood the importance of his innovations and his compositions met with ever increasing disbelief and disapproval, particularly in the period of his advancing deafness. Nonetheless, people did understand that they had the world's greatest living composer in their midst. Prince Lichnowsky, for example, would not allow Beethoven to leave Vienna – though it meant he had to pay the composer a much higher annuity...

Who was this remarkable, unhappy, often sickly, stubborn, often boorish, but also extremely charming musician, who 170 years after his death continues to fascinate music lovers throughout the world? On the basis of a great deal of pictorial material and evidence from his time, we chart the life of Ludwig van Beethoven, one of the world's greatest composers, who fifty–seven years old and as deaf as a post, died on March 26, 1827 in Vienna as the result of pneumonia with complications.

The father of Ludwig van Beethoven, Johann, was nowhere nearly as high on the social ladder as the dignified Leopold Mozart, father and teacher of Wolfgang Amadeus; on the other hand neither were his roots in the countryside, like those of Franz Joseph Haydn's forefathers. He belonged rather to the petit bourgeoisie, and he had only his musical profession to thank for his good contacts with the court in Bonn. Johann had changed the originally Flemish "van" in the family name to "von," but this had nothing to do with aristocratic descent. (Later, Ludwig himself changed it back to the old "van".) Johann's father, also a Ludwig, came from Mechelen. He left there in 1731 to become a choral singer and violinist at the court of Bonn. In order to supplement his meager income he began a wine business; the reason his son learned far too early to enjoy the pleasures of alcohol. Later, he was promoted to Hofkapellmeister.

The family's social status sank again when in 1767, at the age of twenty–seven, Johann married the widow of a master chef. Magdalena Keverich was a sweet, sickly woman, whose husband's lust for drink gave her a great deal to put up with. He lost his job as a tenor in the stadtkapelle, and after Magdalena's death in 1787 left the care of his family in the hands of the young Ludwig. The latter was obliged to provide for them as a violist, while his father spent his time in the taverns.

Ludwig was the eldest of three surviving sons. (Four other children died young.) His brothers Karl (b. 1774) and Johann (b. 1776), eventually made good – as a civil servant and a pharmacist respectively – in Vienna where Ludwig had brought them after he himself had settled there permanently in 1792.

Above right: The luxurious palace where the Electors and Archbishops of Cologne stayed when in Bonn. An engraving by Johann Ziegler (Bonn, Städtiches Kunstmuseum).

A new cultural climate was created in the great centers of Germany as a result of the reforms of Emperor Joseph II.
Right: View of Bonn.

Joseph II with his brother Leopold, who succeeded him in 1790.

Ludwig von Beethoven was born on December 16 or 17, 1770 in Bonn. For a long time, however, his father Johann claimed that his son had come into the world in 1772. In this way, he was able to present a most unusual child prodigy to the court who could perform as a pianist in order to supplement Johann's meager income. In the 18th century child prodigies were not unusual in German–speaking countries where musical tuition began at a very early age. As a so–called five–year–old (but in reality already seven), the young Ludwig was able to compete when he first appeared as a pianist. The uncertainty concerning his age continued until at least 1783, as demonstrated by an article about the court organist Christian Gottlob Neefe, Beethoven's first important music teacher. Neefe was under the impression that the young pianist, who could already play J.S. Bach's *The Well–Tempered Clavier* perfectly and largely from memory, was only eleven years old...

Tuition in piano and organ playing and in composition from the cultured Neefe was extremely important for Ludwig who, apart from comprehensive musical instruction (piano, organ, violin, and viola), had received little general education from his parents. In later life, this problem was to result in his obsessive need for knowledge. Often he also attempted to conceal this deficiency in his development, which sometimes manifested itself in strange or gruff and grumpy behavior.

Musically he made such rapid progress that in 1784 he was appointed assistant organist to Neefe.

Through his friend Franz Gerhard Wegeler, Beethoven made the acquaintance of the Von Breuning family in this period, and he would remain friends with them for the rest of his life. Helène von Breuning was an aristocratic widow who had a great interest in art and music. Beethoven gave piano lessons to her daughter Eleonore and her youngest son Lorenz and experienced the beneficial influence of this cultural environment. Wegeler later married Eleonore. Beethoven continued to be friends with her brother Stephan, and it was the latter's son,

Gerhard, who would comfort the composer in the last days of his life.

In the house of the Von Breunings Beethoven met the young Baroness van Westerholt, who was the first woman to arouse passionate feelings in him.

In 1786 in Bonn a university was founded by the enlightened Elector Maximilian Franz, which was visited by Beethoven for a short time. The climate of openness, the importance attached to philosophy, jurisprudence, classics, and the ideas of the Enlightenment greatly contributed to the forming of the young Beethoven. Even though he was not well enough equipped intellectually to fully understand the complex world of the ideas of Immanuel Kant, he was nonetheless fascinated by this philosopher.

Above: *Portrait of Maria Magdalena Keverich, Beethoven's mother, portrayed in a contemporary engraving.*

A drawing, dating from 1889, of
Bonngasse 55, the house where
Beethoven was born, by R. Bleissel
(Bonn, Beethovenhaus).

Johann van Beethoven, father of
the composer, in a portrait by
Leopold Grass (Vienna,
Historisches Museum der Stadt).

Above: A silhouette from 1782
which represents Madame von
Breuning with her children
Eléonore, Christoph, Lorenz, and
Stephan (Bonn, Beethovenhaus).
Left: Portrait of Baroness von
Westerholt (Bonn,
Beethovenhaus).

In the spring of 1787 Beethoven went to Vienna for the first time, a journey which was probably financed by Elector Maximilian Franz or by another of Beethoven's admirers, Count Waldstein, to whom a piano sonata is dedicated. The intention was that the 17–year–old Ludwig would broaden his musical horizons and at least come into contact with Wolfgang Amadeus Mozart. Unfortunately, nowhere is it clearly recorded that the two geniuses actually did meet. It may well be that Beethoven played for Mozart and perhaps had a few lessons in composition. But Beethoven was forced to abruptly cut short his visit to Vienna – he received a message that his mother's health was failing. He returned to Bonn, where his mother died in July.

Within two years the condition of his father, Johann, also deteriorated. He largely spent his

Vienna seen from the Belvedere Palace, an oil painting by Bernardo Bellotto (Vienna, Kunsthistorisches Museum).

Before Beethoven left Bonn, his friends presented him with a farewell album containing greetings, dedications, and best wishes. Left: A page signed by the brother of Babette Koch, one of Beethoven's dearest lady friends. Below: Count Waldstein, to whom Beethoven dedicated a piano sonata, said farewell with the often-quoted wish: 'May your assiduous labor help you to receive Mozart's spirit from Haydn's hands...'

days in the tavern, and had now lost his job as a singer and been placed under legal restraint. The 19-year-old Ludwig was named head of the family and had to provide for his two brothers. He did this by taking two jobs; he was court organist as well as violist in the court orchestra. This left him little time for composition, but in this period he did become acquainted with the work of various opera composers.

In July 1792 Franz Joseph Haydn, by then 60 years old, visited Bonn on his way back from London to Vienna. Friends of Beethoven showed him the *Cantata on the Death of Emperor Joseph II*. Haydn expressed his admiration of the young composer and advised him to settle in Vienna. At the intervention of Count Waldstein, Beethoven was again given paid leave by the Elector, and on November 2nd or 3rd of that year he left Bonn for good.

View of the Lobkowitzplatz in Vienna, by Bernardo Bellotto (Vienna, Kunsthistorisches Museum). The prince's palace is clearly visible on the left of the painting.

In Vienna Beethoven wished to complete his studies with Haydn, but during the course of 1793 it appeared that the old maestro actually did not have enough time to spare for him. When in January 1794 Haydn again left for London, it gave Beethoven the opportunity to look for another teacher, and he found one in the person of Johann Georg Albrechtsberger, an expert in counterpoint. Furthermore, he was occasionally able to take lessons from Antonio Salieri who, according to gossip which has never been substantiated, had poisoned his rival Mozart out of jealousy. This, because he had been unable to accept that Mozart was more original than he was and had much more success at the Viennese court and with the public in Europe. Beethoven did not get much out of Salieri's lessons; they concerned vocal technique in Italian melodrama (Beethoven only wrote one opera and that was in German) and the art of diplomatic behavior...

Far above: *Beethoven's violin teacher, Franz Ries.*
Above, from left to right: *Joseph Haydn; Ludwig van Beethoven on a miniature by Christian Horneman (Bonn, Beethovenhaus); Ferdinand Ries, son of Beethoven's violin teacher and, in his turn, pupil of the composer (Bonn, Beethovenhaus).*
Left: *Beethoven's viola.*

Beethoven playing the piano for the family of Count Razumowsky.

In 1794 French troops forced Maximilian Franz to leave Bonn. This meant that Beethoven was no longer paid his stipend and was thrown on his own resources to earn an income. Happily, it quickly became apparent that in the Vienna of that period there were countless ways in which a talented young man could step into the limelight. Count Waldstein had already introduced Beethoven into the best circles in Vienna and his gifts as a pianist, especially in the field of improvisation, had attracted much attention. Beethoven was received with open arms by, among others, Prince Joseph Maximilian Lobkowitz, Prince Karl Lichnowsky in whose palace he stayed, Count Razumowsky, Count

From the very start of his stay in Vienna, Beethoven's piano–playing was admired by the public. The "pianoforte," which was so–called because – in contrast to the harpsichord – it could be played both softly ('piano' in Italian) and loudly ("forte" in Italian), was invented in 1709 or 1710 by the harpsichord builder Bartolomeo Cristofori. Taste in the years around 1700 demanded an instrument with more vitality, and Cristofori found the solution in striking the strings instead of plucking them. Below one of Beethoven's pianos (Bonn, Beethovenhaus).
Around 1760, when the instrument had been greatly improved, it began to completely displace its predecessors, the harpsichord and clavichord. At this time the instru-

ment was still called the "Hammerklavier" and, other than the fact that it had a rather metallic sound, it differed from the modern piano in that there was no "mechanical repetition," a device which since 1780 has allowed notes to be repeated very quickly on pianos and grand pianos. During the last few years the original "Hammerklavier" has again gained wide popularity due to an increasing interest in "authentic" performance practice.

Right: *The title page of the three trios for piano, violin, and cello, opus 1 (Vienna, Österreichische Nationalbibliothek).*

Count Razumowsky, the Russian czar's ambassador, was one of Beethoven's most important patrons from the very start of the latter's stay in Vienna. Beethoven dedicated the Fifth Symphony as well as the three Quartets opus 59 to him.
Left a portrait of the count, and below his luxurious palace in Vienna, in a watercolor by Eduard Gurk (Vienna, Historisches Museum der Stadt).

The White Swan tavern in Vienna, where Beethoven met his friends from the music world, a watercolor by Emile Hutter (Vienna, Historisches Museum der Stadt).

Moritz von Fries, Prince Joseph Schwarzenberg, Baron Ignaz Gleichenstein, Countess Maria Wilhelmina Thun, and Baron Gottfried van Swieten, who had once been a close friend of the late Mozart. These names can be found in the works of Beethoven which are dedicated to them. Thanks to these people, Beethoven was able to lead a comfortable life; he even had a horse at his disposal, presented to him by Count Johann von Browne. They put up with his intolerable behavior, at least in the early years, and regarded it as something belonging to the character of a musical genius.

Despite his boorish behavior, Beethoven made many friends among the musicians in Vienna, such as the "music–making count," Zmeskall von Domanowitz; the violinist Ignace Schuppanzigh, who with his famous string quartet performed for Prince Lichnowsky and Count Razumowsky; the mandolin player and violinist Wenzel Krumpholtz; the violinist Ferdinand Ries; and the young Karl Amenda, theologian and fairly good amateur violinist. Amenda, with whom he had become acquainted at the house of Prince Lobkowitz, was his most important conversation partner in matters of philosophy and spirituality. The friends met each other in the White Swan Inn, a hospitable Viennese tavern.

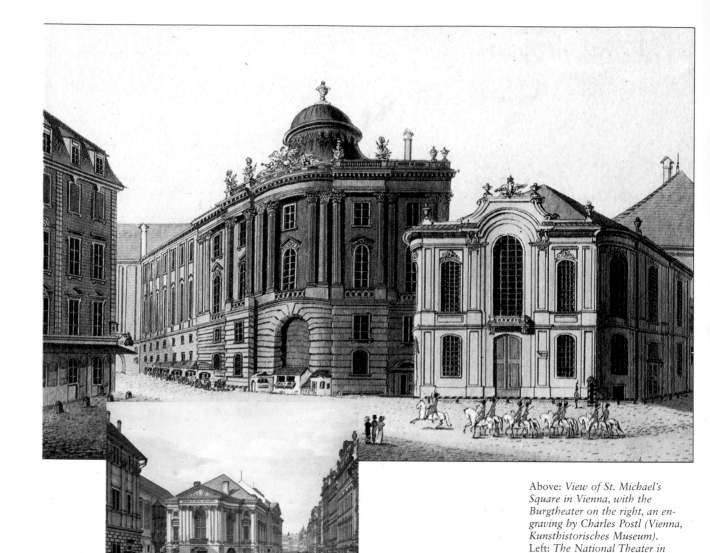

Above: *View of St. Michael's Square in Vienna, with the Burgtheater on the right, an engraving by Charles Postl (Vienna, Kunsthistorisches Museum).*
Left: *The National Theater in Prague, where Beethoven had great success, a watercolor by Vincenz Morstadt (Prague, Municipal Museum).*

On March 29, 1795, in the Burgtheater in Vienna, Beethoven gave his first public concert, in his twin capacity of composer and pianist. Among other things, he performed the *Second Piano Concerto*. The reaction of the critics was mixed. They also had mixed views about Beethoven's first published compositions. The composer's utter willfulness was immediately remarked upon, however.

Between 1796 and 1798 Beethoven undertook a concert tour abroad – for the first and last time. This extremely successful tour took him to Berlin, Leipzig, Dresden, Prague, Presberg (nowadays Bratislava), and Budapest.

In Vienna in the last years of the 18th century, Beethoven began to be regarded as the most important successor to Mozart (who died in 1791) and Haydn (who by this time was elderly). After all, before 1800 Beethoven wrote and published the following works: the *First Symphony, three Trios op. 1 for piano, violin, and cello*; the first 16 *Piano Sonatas*, among which was the extremely important *Pathétique* (op. 13), at that time Beethoven's most advanced work; the first three *Sonatas op. 12 for violin and piano*; the two *Sonatas op. 5 for cello and piano*; the six *Quartets op. 18*; the beautiful *Quintet op. 16*, after a composition by Mozart for piano and wind instruments; and the first two *Piano Concertos*. In addition, he wrote a great deal of chamber music, such as *Septet op. 20*, variations, rondos, and ballet music. His

Knight's Ballet, for example, had already been composed in Bonn, when Count Waldstein was appointed a Knight of Malta. Furthermore, the greatest part of his music for wind instruments had already been written (*Octet op. 103, Sextet op. 71*), as had a number of arias in the Italian melodramatic style (*Ah, perfido!, op. 65*, to a libretto by Metastasio) and lieder, including the *Adelaide cycle, op. 46*.

In the last years of the 18th century Beethoven lived on the Graben, on the third floor of number 241. Below: View of the Graben, an engraving by C. Schütz (Vienna, Historisches Museum).

Around 1800, Beethoven began to notice the first symptoms of hearing loss; within two decades this would lead to total deafness. His friends Amenda and Wegeler were the first he told, in two poignant letters in June 1801. In these letters he also expanded upon his relationship with God and with other people. He wrote to Amenda (the theologian): "Your friend Beethoven is unhappy; he is living in a state of war with nature and with the Creator. I have cursed Him many times, who abandons his creatures to their fate, so that at the slightest provocation the most beautiful flower withers, or is broken". And to Wegener: "Often I have damned the Creator and my own existence. Through Plutarch I have arrived at resignation. As far as possible I want to meet my fate with head held high, though there will be moments in my life when I shall be God's most unhappy creature."

In 1793, the Italian Salvatore Viganò, the most important choreographer of the 18th century, came to live in Vienna. He did the choreography for Beethoven's ballet *The Creatures of Prometheus*, the premiere of which was on March 28, 1801 in the Burgtheater in Vienna and which, like other work by Viganò, had great success.

Viganò was also himself a ballet dancer and the inventor of "choreodrama," a performance with dramatic content in which all expression was translated by the dance. In 1813 Viganò received an appointment with La Scala in Milan, to which he remained tied until his death in 1821. His first production was Beethoven's *Prometheus*, but the ballet now underwent sweeping changes – music by Haydn, Mozart, and Viganò himself being added.

The piano sonatas which Beethoven had already written before 1802 showed a very clear break in style compared with the sonatas of Haydn and Mozart. The piano for which Beethoven was writing (at first the "Hammerklavier") already had properties which might be compared to those of the modern-day piano; while Mozart and Haydn adopted, as it were, the harpsichord technique on the recently invented piano, which externally looked very much like a harpsichord but which sounded totally different. In a harpsichord the notes are short, so that speed and dexterity are of extreme importance. In the piano, which evolved rapidly in Beethoven's time, the emphasis lies more on great resonance, on powerfully executed virtuoso passages, and on the opportunity to achieve various gradations in volume, from a soft whisper (pedal!) to deafeningly loud. This is also one of the reasons why in Beethoven's time the piano was the concert-going public's favorite instrument.

Because Beethoven himself was an extremely good pianist, with a great talent for improvisation, in his compositional work he was able to exploit the possibilities of this new instrument to their fullest. A completely new form of the piano sonata was created, in which he also often added a fourth part, a minuet or a scherzo. *The Sonatas op. 2* and *op. 7* are good examples of this. In the *Grand Sonata, "Pathétique," op. 13*, Beethoven's entire genius is revealed – musical ideas, a richness of form, and an elegaic composition forged together into a synthesis which endeavors to express optimism and the victory of positive powers.

In Beethoven's early period, therefore, the piano was the most important instrument, while for orchestra and quartet he still composed in the traditional 18th-century style, though in these works, too, his self-will and urge for innovation can be found.

After Salvatore Viganò stopped dancing he devoted himself completely to choreography, working at La Scala in Milan, where he also staged Beethoven's Prometheus *(Contempory etching, Milan, Civica Raccolta Bertarelli).*

The interior of the Burgtheater in Vienna, where on March 28th, 1801 Beethoven's ballet music The Creatures of Prometheus, *choreographed by the famous Italian dancer and choreographer Salvatore Viganò, was premiered (Anonymous contemporary etching, Vienna, Historisches Museum der Stadt).*

Around 1802, Beethoven began to realize that his deafness would become worse and would remain incurable. In October of that year this knowledge plunged him into a deep depression and he wrote a letter, intended for his friends and his two brothers, which is known as the "testament of Heiligenstadt". He had returned to Heiligenstadt, a small village near Vienna, some time before because he had been forced to reduce the number of his public performances and longed for seclusion. The document is dated October 6, 1802 and shows his desperation about a complaint that "...would still have to be borne if I had another profession, but which for me means utter horror," as he wrote to his friend Wegener.

"Oh, Deity, you can see into my soul, you know it; you know that here inside lies a love for the future and a readiness to do good. Oh, people, if you ever read these words, then think

View of the church of Heiligenstadt, the village near Vienna to which Beethoven, depressed, returned in the summer and autumn of 1802 (Etching by Lorenz Janscha, Vienna, Historisches Museum der Stadt).

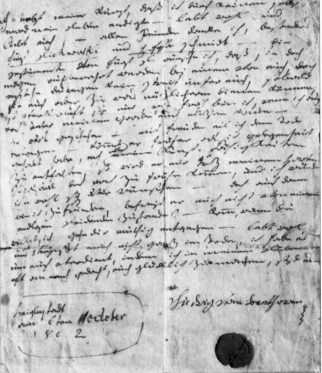

that you have judged me unjustly and that this unhappy one is only happy to find a fellow human being who, despite the impediments of his nature, has done everything which lay in his power to be accepted among artists and honorable men."

Despite his dejection, in that year Beethoven succeeded in completing his *Second Symphony*. Remarkably, there is barely anything in this work which reflects the deep gloom which he revealed in his letters.

There has been much speculation about the cause of Beethoven's deafness. Nowadays it is no longer accepted that syphilis or alcoholism played a role, as had been claimed earlier. It is more probable that he suffered from a form of skin tuberculosis which also affected his immune response system. This explains why he was sickly (inherited from his mother's side?) and aged prematurely.

Above left: *View of Heilingenstadt, a watercolor by Tobie Paulino (Vienna, Historisches Museum).*

Above right: *The last page of the letter known as "The Heiligenstadt Testament" (Hamburg, Universitätsbibliothek).*

*Napoleon at the St. Bernhard pass,
by Jaques–Louis David (Versailles,
Musée de la Château).*

Above: *Beethoven at the age of 36, in an 1806 portrait attributed to Isodoro Neugaas. The first performance of Beethoven's* Third Symphony *took place in the An der Wien theater in 1805.*

Above right: *A view of part of the theater's auditorium, a contemporary engraving (Vienna, Historisches Museum).*

At the beginning of the 19th century, Beethoven demonstrated a naïve sympathy for Napoleon Bonaparte, seeing in him a sort of "pure" hero who wanted the best for "his" people. Thus, he dedicated his *Third Symphony* the (*Eroica*) to the first consul of an imaginary republic based on the Roman model. But then, before the symphony was published, Napoleon had himself crowned emperor, and Beethoven removed his dedication and replaced it with the much more general "in memory of a great man" – a person of enlightened ideas. To Beethoven, an emperor was the equivalent of a tyrant. Eventually he dedicated the symphony to Prince Lobkowitz.

While the *First* and *Second Symphonies* owed a great deal to Mozart and Haydn, in the *Third*, composed between 1802 and 1804, Beethoven went to work in a revolutionary manner. He replaced the traditional minuet as the third movement with a scherzo, obtaining a unity which was not based on old musical structures, but which stemmed directly from his musical *idea*: to bring across an ideological message structured around the person of a "great man," an enlightened hero.

After the *Third Symphony* Beethoven began to work on the *Fifth*. In the summer of 1806 he

On December 22, 1808, Beethoven's Fifth was performed for the first time in the An der Wien theater, together with the Sixth (Pastoral) (anonymous engraving, Vienna, Historisches Museum).

Left: The first page of the manuscript of the Fifth Symphony (Berlin, Staatsbibliotheek). Under the second measure we can read Beethoven's annotation, "Flutes, Oboe, Clarinets, Bassoons, Horns, all obligato."

interrupted this in order to start on the *Fourth*, which was performed for the first time in May 1807, in Prince Lobkowitz's palace. In this symphony the composer returned temporarily to the trusted forms and structures of Haydn's time, a sort of belated tribute. However, in his further work on the *Fifth* (1804–1808) Beethoven once again used the revolutionary principles of the *Third*. He dubbed the beginning of the symphony "Fate knocking at the door."

A suggestive, pastoral landscape by the English artist John Constable, a contemporary of Beethoven (Dedham Mill; London, Victoria & Albert Museum; detail).

Here we must think not so much of Beethoven's own fate, but rather of that which is dark and threatening in the world and which can only be resisted by reason. The *Fifth*, therefore, is about all people, all who are searching for liberation and happiness. It was dedicated to the composer's two patrons, Prince Lobkowitz and Count Razumowsky, who were friends.

The *Sixth Symphony* (*Pastoral*) is the only one which the composer provided with precise descriptions of the separate movements. The first movement is announced as "Awakening of happy feelings on arriving in the countryside," the second as "Scene by the brook." Up to this point the symphony is fairly traditional in form. But then follow not two separate movements, such as a scherzo and finale, for example, but one long movement which is divided into three parts: "Peasant's merry–making" (also called "Merry gathering of country folk"), "The storm" (also called "Storm and Tempest" or "Thunderstorm"), and "Happy and thankful feelings after the storm." Because of these descriptions and its anomalous structure, this symphony is very different from the symphonies preceding and following it. It also refers to the future; for example, Beethoven indicated beforehand the rich ideas which Gustav Mahler managed to express in his symphonies.

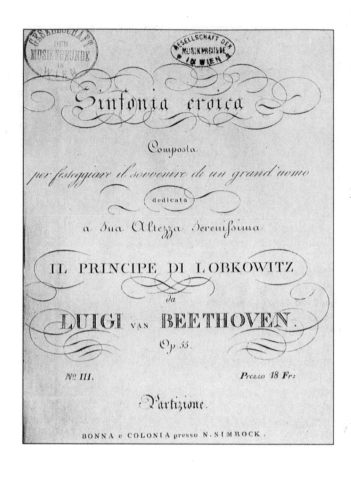

 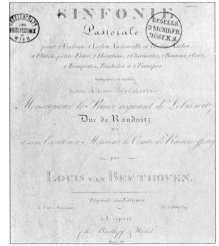

Right: *Two preliminary pages from scores of the* Sixth Symphony *(Pastoral). That on the right has a dedication to Prince Lobkowitz and Count Razumowsky.*

Above right: *Preliminary page from a score of the* Third Symphony *(Eroica).*

Left: *Thérèse, one of the two most important women in the composer's life, with (above left) Joséphine von Brunswick.*

Above right: *Beethoven also fostered amorous feelings for Giulietta Guicciardi, to whom he dedicated the* Moonlight Sonata. *(Anonymous miniature, Bonn, Beethovenhaus.)*

In addition to intense friendships, Beethoven also had a passionate love life, many details of which have far from surfaced. In 1799, through his friend Zmeskall, Beethoven became acquainted with the Von Brunswick family and the daughters Thérèse and Joséphine. This noble family possessed estates in Hungary, and like other wealthy Austro–Hungarian families, spent much time in Vienna. Beethoven, at that time not yet thirty, also became acquainted with a young cousin of the Von Brunswick sisters, Giulietta Guicciardi, to whom he found himself strongly attracted.

Nevertheless, after he had become the family's music teacher, he also courted both the sisters. And at the end of 1803 Giulietta Guicciardi ended up marrying Count Wenzel Robert Gallenberg. Beethoven had dedicated the *Moonlight Sonata* to this great love and later, in

strange circumstances, he would meet her again. In 1821, ruined by a profligate life in Naples, Giulietta and her husband returned to Vienna and Giulietta asked the composer to lend her 500 florins...

In the meantime, Beethoven had further cultivated Joséphine (nicknamed "Pepi"), but this was going too far for the Von Brunswick family; he was a famous musician, true, but he was still a commoner. Joséphine married Count Joseph Deym. He died in 1803, and the family again had to intervene to forbid the love between Beethoven and Joséphine. Here begins an unsolved mystery in Beethoven's life. A famous letter, which Beethoven sent to an "immortal beloved," has survived. It has always been assumed that he was referring to Thérèse von Brunswick. Until her death in 1861, she maintained that the letter was addressed to her on the

occasion of a secret and platonic engagement between the two. Probably she herself came to believe this during all those years, but several biographers are of the opinion that matters were very different from what the noble old Hungarian lady would have us believe. In their opinion, the letter was written not in 1806, but in June 1812 in Teplitz, and it was addressed to Joséphine and not Thérèse. And, as other facts indicate, it was certainly not platonic.

In 1812, more than nine months before the birth of her daughter Minona, Joséphine had been deserted by her second husband, Baron Cristoph von Stackelberg. Minona was born on April 9, 1813, so Beethoven (think of his non–platonic letter of June 1812) might very well have been the father of the girl. The latter, by the way, later suppressed the correspondence between Beethoven and her mother. Furthermore, until her death in 1821 Joséphine lived cut off from her family, perhaps even disowned. The true course of events, therefore, was suppressed, with Beethoven's consent, in order to cause no offence in higher circles.

The Sonata opus 27 *has a certain Ludwig Rellstab to thank for its happily–chosen name,* Moonlight Sonata. *The andante aroused feelings in Rellstab which he compared to the moonlight reflected in a mountain lake, exactly as in this painting by Joseph Wright of Derby, (detail, New Haven, Yale Center for British Art).*

Left: *Detail of a painting of Teresa Malfatti at the piano, the "bourgeoise" whom Beethoven almost married (private collection).*

Prince Lichnowsky's castle in Grätz, in a contemporary painting.

The woman who Beethoven came closest to marrying was Teresa Malfatti. He had a relationship with her in 1809–1810. There were also amorous involvements with Countess Erdödy, the singer Amalia Seebald, and the writer Bettina Brentano. There are various reasons why none of these relationships seemed to last very long. The women who interested him were often unobtainable because of class differences, or because they were already married. Furthermore, Beethoven's obstinate nature, his disorderliness, and his obsession with composing stood in the way.

Beethoven moved some 30 times while in Vienna, living as a sort of gypsy in great disorder, often making trouble with his patrons and their staff, and dressing badly. For a long time he occupied an apartment in the palace of his patron, Prince Lichnowsky from whom he also received an annual allowance of 600 florins. But in 1806, he came into conflict with this patron as well, in the latter's summer residence in Grätz. Lichnowsky had asked him to give a concert for a few French guests. Beethoven stubbornly refused, made a scene, and lost both his apartment and his allowance.

Above left: *Johann Wolfgang Goethe, in an etching from the "Sturm und Drang" period (Naples, Museo di S. Martino).*
Above right top: *Johann Gottfried Herder, in a portrait by Anton Graff (Alberstadt, Gleinhaus).*
Above right bottom: *Friedrich Schiller, in an etching by Anton Graff (Berlin, Staatliche Museen).*

Beethoven was influenced by the "Sturm und Drang" movement, as were many of his contemporaries. It was a cultural, largely literary, movement which arose in Germany between 1770 and 1780. Its leading lights, such as Johann Wolfgang Goethe, Johann Gottfried Herder, and Friedrich Schiller, strove not only for a revolution in aesthetic values, but also aimed at a (difficult to realize) philosophical, political, and social revolution. Their ideas echo the thoughts of philosophers such as Leibniz and Spinoza, as well as the criticism of Jean Jacques Rousseau of rationalism, which had arisen by then. The "genius" of the artist (Shakespeare, for example) played an important role in the forming of their theories, as did a return to "nature." This new synthesis placed "Sturm und Drang" somewhere between the Enlightenment and the Romantic Movement. It was the first avant–garde movement in European history.

After the creative explosion of the *Fourth*, *Fifth*, and *Sixth Symphonies*, Beethoven found himself back in Vienna, living alone after his row with Prince Lichnowsky, and more and more often in conflict with other patrons due to his unpredictable behavior – which undoubtedly had a great deal to do with his advancing deafness. In this period he created the *Concerto for violin and orchestra*, which was dedicated to his good friend and pupil, Stephan Breuning. The concerto was written for the well–known violinist Franz Clement, who played it on December 13, 1806, in the An der Wien theater.

Apart from the fact that Beethoven was vulnerable to creative torment on a personal level, as already described, he was also affected by the powerful political events of his day. In 1797 and 1801 Austria was defeated by France and forced to concede a considerable amount of territory. After the Battle of Austerlitz (December 2, 1805), the severe conditions of the Treaty of Presburg came to the fore. Napoleon had formed a federation of Rhine States, which posed a threat to the Empire. The Emperor was further humiliated by Napoleon's fresh victories, and only when the great statesman Metternich became Chancellor in 1809 did Austria (with the Congress of Vienna, 1814) regain some of its influence on the European stage.

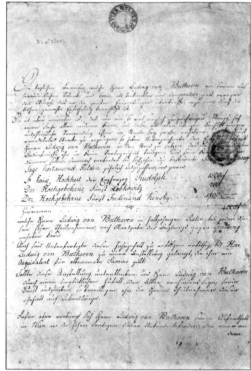

Above left: *King Jérôme
Bonaparte of Westphalia, in a
painting by Antoine–Jean Gros.*
Above right: *The contract ensuring
Beethoven an annual income of
4,000 florins.*

In October 1808, some time after his break
with Prince Lichnowsky, Beethoven received an
offer from the court of Kassel to enter the service of the King of Westphalia, Jerôme
Bonaparte, the brother of Napoleon, for whom
the new kingdom had been created. From a letter of January 7, 1809, to his publisher Breitkopf
it appears that Beethoven had already decided to
go. "...Because of all sorts of intrigues, machina-
tions, and my destitution I am finally forced to
leave the German fatherland, which is still uni-
que of its sort. I have accepted the offer of His
Majesty the King of Westphalia to enter his

service as bandmaster for an annual salary of 600 golden ducats.... I have just sent a letter by post in which I have confirmed that I am coming and I am now only waiting for my letter of appointment in order to make preparations for the journey."

In the meantime, friends of the composer tried to prevent his departure. Count Ignaz Gleichenstein and Countess Anna Maria Erdödy requested Prince Kinsky, Prince Lobkowitz, and Archduke Rudolph of Habsburg to grant Beethoven an annual allowance. On March 1, 1809, a document which can be regarded as the first legal contract of patronage was drawn up. This is a highly remarkable contract which laid relatively few obligations on Beethoven. There is no seal on it, however, because before it was due to come into effect and before Beethoven received his first annual 4,000 florins, the three contributors had to leave Vienna as it was about to be invaded by the French. Then, in 1811 Lobkowitz was placed under legal restraint, and in 1812 Kinsky died after he fell from his horse. It was only after 1815 and a long legal battle that Beethoven received what was due to him.

Beethoven remained good friends with the third benefactor in the contract, partly because Archduke Rudolph was his pupil for a long time. A number of important compositions are dedicated to him: the two last *Piano Concertos*, the two *Sonatas, opus* 80, "*Les Adieux*" and *opus* 106 "*Hammerklavier*," the *Trio, opus* 97, "*Archduke*," the *Missa Solemnis* and the *Great fugue, opus* 133 for string quartet. Besides a friendship of many years, these works also show Beethoven's respect for the tradition that dictated that complex and virtuoso compositions were dedicated to high–ranking personages.

The three great admirers of Beethoven who signed the contract: from top to bottom, Archduke Rudolf, Prince Kinsky, and Prince Lobkowitz.

The contract which Beethoven negotiated with the Princes Lobkowitz and Kinsky and Archduke Rudolf contained, among others, the following paragraphs:

2. Beethoven shall still retain the right to make journeys in relation to his art because only in this way can he acquire reputation and achieve a certain prosperity.

3. His dearest wish, in due course, is to actively enter into service of the Emperor so that, due to his fixed honorarium, he can give up the present annual allowance.

4. Seeing that from time to time Beethoven wishes to present works to a wide public, he would like the assurance from the management of the court theater that every year on Palm Sunday in the An der Wien theater he might conduct an "academy" (performance) at his own expense. In exchange, Beethoven promises to give a charity concert for the poor every year, or, if he himself is unable to conduct, to reserve one of his new works for charity...

In 1809 Napoleon's troops bombarded Vienna again and occupied the city. It was also the year in which Beethoven wrote his Fifth Piano Concerto (Emperor), *and the contract with his three patrons was drawn up (Vienna, Historisches Museum).*

On July 15, 1812, Beethoven returned to the health resort of Teplitz, to the north of Prague. A few days later Johann Wolfgang von Goethe, with his "musical advisor" Karl Friedrich Zelter, also arrived there, and the meeting of the two titans took place. This came about through the mediation of a mutual female friend, the German writer Bettina Brentano. Beethoven and Goethe had previously corresponded about Goethe's play *Egmont*, for which Beethoven had written music, including the *Overture*, which is still played frequently.

Even after they had met several times, there appeared to be little sympathy between the composer and the writer, although their admiration for each other did not diminish. Beethoven's admiration was perhaps greater than that of Goethe. Probably the latter could not divorce the tempestuous, sometimes agressive, music he so admired from Beethoven's personality, which little resembled Goethe's ideal image of an artist. "I have never met an artist who is so concentrated, so energetic and so profound," wrote Goethe about Beethoven, but also: "I am confounded by his talent; he is, however, a completely unrestrained personality who is surely not wrong to detest the world, but in this way he does not make things more pleasant, either for himself or for others." In his turn, Beethoven, in reference to the functions he fulfilled at the court of Weimar, remarked that Goethe loved life at court more than was fitting for a poet.

Below: *Goethe dictating in his study, a year before his death.*

Right: *Beethoven in 1804, while composing the Eroica.*

Though in 1804 Beethoven had still wanted to dedicate his *Third Symphony* to Napoleon, in 1812 and 1814 he wrote "anti–Napoleonic" cantatas, out of joy at the defeats the armies of the French tyrant were then suffering. In 1814, he wrote the cantata *The Victory of Wellington*, which was performed with great success that year in Vienna in a program which also included the premiere of the *Seventh Symphony*. A year later, Napoleon was defeated hopelessly at Waterloo, after which Louis XVIII again took his place on the throne. Beethoven's attitude was not all that politically colored, because in fact the course followed by the new Chancellor, Metternich, was essentially conservative, but stemmed from a natural need for progress and an abhorrence of tyranny, which he translated in his work. In his time, practical politics in

German–speaking countries was reserved to the higher circles. An artist could only become involved as an intellectual and moral mentor.

Thus, Beethoven's symphonies attempt to demonstrate that after a long and dramatic struggle, positive forces overcome the negative ones. Indeed, in all Beethoven's later work a similar optimistic "message" can be recognized. After 1815, a particular aspect of this is still

The naturalistic atmosphere in the Third Symphony *is characterized by the theme of the three horns, which urge on the hunt.* Above: Flourish of Horns', *a painting by Vittorio Amedeo Cignaroli (Zurich, Castle).*

clearer – a mystic element and an interest in the transcendental are strongly present in the last quartets, the last five piano sonatas, the *Ninth Symphony* and the *Missa Solemnis*.

In the *Seventh* and *Eighth Symphonies* (1812), Beethoven again returned to the classical form. As far as content is concerned both symphonies appear to contain less "message" than those previous. Wagner called the *Seventh* the "apothosis of dance," because of its many variations on dance rhythms. In the *Eighth* Beethoven seems to have lost his interest in the symphony form. In this he composed a last, sometimes ironic,

tribute to the style of old masters such as Haydn. In the second movement, for example, he quoted his own humorous canon on Johann Nepomuk Mälzel, a smart businessman who had popularized the metronome. Beethoven regarded the gadget as a symbol of rigid 18th–century musical structures.

It took ten years before Beethoven returned to the symphony form, with his *Ninth Symphony*, that incomparable, monumental, and innovative masterwork which became a milestone in European symphonic music.

Beethoven wrote only one opera, *Fidelio*, although he did consider other theater projects. He had to rework the original version, *Léonore*, three times before everyone was satisfied with the opera, and so four overtures were created – *Léonore 1*, *Léonore 2*, *Léonore 3*, and the *Fidelio Overture*. Although the second is at least as impressive, it is the third that is most played as a separate orchestral work.

Beethoven's other work for the theater is limited to a ballet by Viganò, *The Creatures of Prometheus* and a few individual overtures or scene music for theater.

Fidelio was composed in the form of a *Singspiel*, in which the words are alternatively sung and spoken as, for example, in Mozart's *The Magic Flute*. The moral in the libretto is typical of Beethoven – marital virtue and ideals of freedom are rewarded while wickedness and dereliction of duty are punished. Besides the *Singspiel*, the form of this opera is also related to the French "opéra–comique," in particular the "opéra–de–sauvetage." The most important element of this is the "happy ending" – when all appears to be lost and evil is about to win, something happens which reverses the situation. The popularity of this genre in France had a great deal to do with the insecurity people felt during the Terror period.

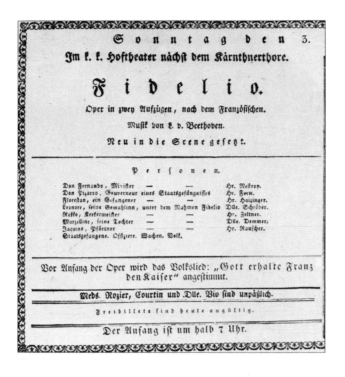

Above: *The original version of* Fidelio (Léonore) *was first performed in the An der Wien theater (left) on November 20, 1805. It was a great fiasco. The final version of the opera was staged in 1814 and was better received by the public.* Above: *The poster announcing this performance.*

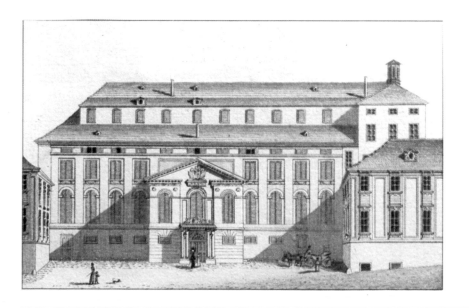

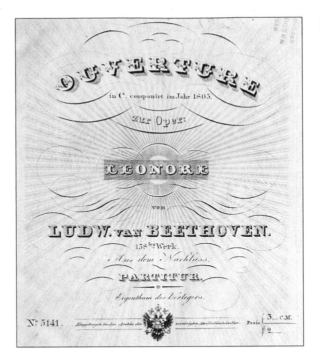

The libretto was based on a play by the
Frenchman Jean Nicolas Bouilly, *Léonore ou
l'amour conjugal,* which itself was based on an
event that actually occurred during the Terror.
Besides Beethoven, the Italian Ferdinando Paër
and Simon Mayr, German in origin, also used
the story for an opera. These two were premiered in Dresden in 1804 and Padua in 1805
respectively (that is to say shortly before
Beethoven's version was first performed in
Vienna on November 20, 1805). It is improbable
that Beethoven knew Paër's or Mayr's music.

Fidelio or conjugal love was performed with
the overture *Léonore 2* (the failed *Léonore 1*
was never performed in Beethoven's lifetime)
and met with such a negative reception that after
three days performances were suspended. The
much–too–long work was shortened to two acts
by Beethoven's friend Stephan von Breuning and
provided with a "better" overture (*Léonore 3*).
On March 29, 1806 the opera was again premiered under the new title *Léonore or The
triumph of conjugal love.* Again it was a fiasco
and after a few performances Beethoven was
forced to withdraw the work. After an extensive
reworking of both the libretto (by Georg

Friedrich Treitschke) and the music, on May 24, 1814 a performance of *Fidelio* was given in the Karinthian Gate theater. Because the overture was still not ready, Beethoven used another – *The Ruins of Athens*. (In later performances the proper overture was indeed played.) This time the opera enjoyed enormous success.

The story takes place in Seville, where Florestan languishes in an underground dungeon, imprisoned by the wily governor of the fort, Pizarro, his personal enemy. Léonore, Florestan's wife, dresses as a young man in order to get into the fort and as "Fidelio" becomes one of the guards. Their commander is the ancient Rocco, a good–natured and sympathic character. In a comical sub–plot (as often in Singspiel) Marzelline, Rocco's daughter, who has not seen through the disguise, falls in love with Fidelio and, in so doing, arouses the jealousy of Jaquino, another warder, who is enamored of her. In the second act Pizarro wants to murder Florestan, but Fidelio threatens Pizarro with a pistol. Then an envoy from the king arrives; Florestan and Fidelio are saved; Pizarro is arrested. All's well that ends well.

In Beethoven's time musical performances no longer remained limited to the court. There was a far greater public for concerts, as witnessed by this painting by G.M. Terrini which depicts a nocturnal concert in the square of the Cascine in Florence.

Beethoven enjoyed working in the big garden of Schloss Schönbrun, here in an etching after a painting by Lorenz Janscha (Vienna, Historisches Museum der Stadt). The first version of Fidelio (Léonore) was conceived in this garden.

After a short siege French troops entered Vienna on November 10th 1805, a few days before the premiere of Léonore. The entry of the "Grande Armée" is seen here in a contemporary print.

The definitive version of the opera contains two elements that Beethoven wished to give special emphasis to in his music – first Léonore's love and the exceptional courage and faith she showed in liberating her husband, Florestan. And second, the injustice of Florestan's imprisonment, his liberation, and Pizarro's punishment, all in accordance with Beethoven's ethical principles.

Although Beethoven, together with dramatist Franz Grillpazer among others, examined various theatrical projects to see if he could use them, his output in this genre stopped with *Fidelio*. He did, however, write various overtures for plays, such as Goethe's *Egmont*, H.J. von Collin's *Coriolanus* and A. von Kotzebue's *The Ruins of Athens* and *King Stephan*.

The fact that Beethoven was an obdurate moralist can be seen from his behavior at the house of his brother, Johann. The latter, having earned a great deal of money as a pharmacist and businessman, had bought a country house in Gneixendorf, where he lived with a certain Thérèse Obeymeyer as his common–law wife. Beethoven became so incensed at this that he threatened to call in the judicial and church authorities. Johann and Thérèse had no alternative but to marry officially.

The music room Beethoven's brother Johann's house in Gneixendorf. Beethoven stayed here with his adopted nephew, Karl.

The hall of the Royal Palace where Beethoven's famous concert for the Congress of Vienna took place in November 1814. This watercolor by Joseph Schütz shows the hall during a masked ball (Vienna, Historisches Museum der Stadt).

Left: *Sketches of Beethoven by Johann Peter Lyser (Bonn, Beethovenhaus).*

The years 1814 and 1815 were tragic for Beethoven in his personal life, although in public life he achieved triumphs with concerts on the occasion of the Congress of Vienna. His other brother, Karl, died in 1815 at the age of forty–one and Beethoven decided to adopt his son, also named Karl, a decision which would lead to great problems. He was not on good terms with his brother's wife, Johanna Reiss, the daughter of a paperhanger. Beethoven, who could be extremely snobbish, looked down on her and compared her to the Queen of the Night, the wicked mother in Mozart's opera *The Magic Flute*. Conflicts arose because in a codicil (false, according to Beethoven) father Karl had left the care of the child to the two of them.

Because of these conflicts Beethoven decided to try to remove the boy from his mother's power. He finally succeeded in doing so in 1820 and at the age of nine Karl went to boarding school.

The Congress of Vienna was organized by Prussia, Russia, Austria, and England to discuss how new borders should be drawn after the defeat of Napoleon. During the Congress, which was held from October 8, 1814 until June 9, 1815, all sorts of events took place, including masked balls, theatrical performances, and concerts. For months, every day was a party in Vienna. Important friends of Beethoven, such as Prince Razumowsky and Archduke Rudolph organized receptions for him where he was introduced to yet more highly–placed persons. In

The Enchanted Castle *by Francis Danby (London, Victoria & Albert Museum). In Beethoven's time his music was often associated with this type of romantic image, which desired to express something about the "condition humaine."*

November 1814, Beethoven conducted a concert consisting of the *Seventh Symphony*, the cantata *The Glorious Moment*, which had been specially composed for this event, and *The Victory of Wellington* for a select audience of dignitaries. The concert was such an enormous success that it was repeated in January 1815. It was to be Beethoven's last concert, because his rapidly worsening deafness made it impossible for him to continue conducting. He eventually became completely deaf in 1819. His deafness probably was partly the reason for his completely unpredictable behavior. His life was increasingly chaotic, he continued to change lodgings, continued to change his staff, and antagonized one friend after another.

In the last twelve years of his life Beethoven was aided by a devoted, though not too bright, friend, Anton Schindler. This lawyer, who had gone into music, had the words "Friend of Beethoven" printed on his calling card... He functioned as a sort of secretary and general factotum, and after Beethoven's death he received control of the 400 notebooks in which the composer kept his daily life up to date. From 1819, the year in which Beethoven became completely deaf, until 1827, the year of his death, such notebooks were the only link between Beethoven and the outside world. Besides questions from countless conversation partners, they contain the composer's thoughts, accounts, book titles, and often also musical ideas.

Unfortunately, Schindler was not immune to the criticism that Beethoven did not spare him and destroyed about two thirds of the notebooks which contained offensive remarks about himself and others. In 1845, there were only 137 notebooks left and these, together with musical sketches, letters and annotations were entrusted to the Royal Library in Berlin. This concerns some 11,000 pages which contain everything from banal everyday activities to important political or literary events. Schindler also wrote a biography of Beethoven in which he rendered his inept interpretations of the maestro's work. For years this biography obscured insight into the actual musical intentions of the composer.

A portrait of Beethoven by Ferdinand Waldmüller, 1823 (Berlin, Nationalbibliothek).

Beethoven wrote five piano concertos, but only one violin concerto, besides Triple Concerto *for piano, violin, cello and orchestra. The works which are now called the* First Piano Concerto *and the* Second Piano Concerto *were actually written in reverse order. In the* Third Piano Concerto *Beethoven tried to give voice to the same ideas from the Enlightenment as in his symphonies – dramatic conflicts followed by the victory of Good. For unknown reasons the* Fifth Piano Concerto *acquired the name* Emperor Concerto. *It demands extreme virtuosity on the part of the pianist.*
Beethoven also made a transcription for piano of the Violin Concerto, *opus 61.*

In addition to piano concertos Beethoven also wrote a large number of piano sonatas which have nicknames such as Pathétique, Pastoral, Waldstein, Hammerklavier, *and* Appassionata.
The dramatic character of the Appassionata *sonata reminded Beethoven's pupil Carl Czerny of a storm at sea and distant calls for help. Here is* Shipwreck, *a painting by Philip Jakob de Loutherbourg.*

Below: *The first page of the 1st movement (Allegro) of the* Appassionata *sonata (Paris, Bibliothèque Nationale).*

Angels singing and playing, by Jan van Eyck (Ghent, St. Bavo).

The two most important compositions of the last years of Beethoven's life were both written for chorus, soloists, and orchestra. In the *Ninth Symphony* (*Choral*), 1822–1824 and the *Missa Solemnis* (1819–1823), Beethoven's experience of life and his fully crystallized musical ideas form a marvellous synthesis. Originally, there was no singing in the *Ninth Symphony*. Beethoven wrote the work on commission from the London Philharmonic Society and did not add the last movement with the sections for chorus and soloists until the end, after many doubts. For this movement he took the text from Schiller's "Ode to Joy" as his starting point. The

symphony was performed for the first time on May 7, 1824 in the Karinthian Gate theater. The chorus had been rehearsed by, among others, Beethoven's friend Ignaz Shuppanzigh, since the composer had been as deaf as a post for some years. At the concert – which was a huge success – the "Kyrie," "Credo" and "Agnus Dei" from the *Missa Solemnis* were played, as well as the *Overture, opus* 124.

The ode "An die Freude" was written in 1785 by the German writer Friedrich Schiller and published a year later in the journal *Thalia*. The work expresses typical 18th–century ideas, with universal happiness as its theme. By "Joy" a brotherhood of all people is meant here, people who actually enjoy the abundance of life in a universe buttressed by the harmony of Reason.

Beethoven made some changes in the poem, added one or two stanzas, left a few stanzas out, changed the order and fitted the whole into his specific musical ideas for the *Ninth Symphony*. The interaction of the chorus and orchestra, as Schiller had intended it, was modified. The whole still has a devastating effect on new generations of listeners. The thought that this masterwork, like the *Missa Solemnis*, was composed by someone who was deaf and therefore could never hear the music himself, is at once both amazing and terribly sad.

Autograph of the "Ode to Joy" from the Ninth Symphony. *Above left is written "Allegro Energico e sempre ben mercate le note". At the bottom of the page the famous opening words can be recognized – "Seid umschlungen, Millionen!"*

PROGRESS	TEMPI	PERFORMERS	LYRICS
recitative	mezzoforte	baritone solo	O friends, not these sounds! Rather let us sing something more pleasant and more joyful!
allegro assai	forte	baritone solo strings (piano) hobo clarinet	1 Joy, thou spark from flame immortal 2 Daughter of Elysium! 3 Drunk with fire, O heav'n-born Goddess, 4 We invade thy halidom! 5 Let thy magic bring together 6 All whom earth-born laws divide; 7 All mankind shall be as brothers 8 'Neath thy tender wings and wide.
		chorus	Repetition verse 5-8
	piano	tenor, baritone, alto, soli	9 He that's had that best good fortune, 10 To his friend a friend to be 11 He that's won a noble woman, 12 Let him join our jubilee! 13 Ay, and who a single other 14 Soul on earth can call his own; 15 But let him who ne'er achieved it 16 Steal away in tears alone.
	forte	chorus	Repetition verse 13-16
	piano	baritone and tenor, soli, then alto, finally soprano	17 Joy doth every living creature 18 Draw from Nature's ample breast; 19 All good men and all those evil 20 Follow on her roseate quest. 21 Kisses doth she give, and vintage, 22 Friends who firm in death have stood; 23 Joy of life the worm receiveth, 24 And the angels dwell with God!
	forte	chorus	Repetition verse 21-24
lento	fortissimo	chorus	Repetition verse 24
allegro assai alla marcia	mezzoforte	tenor solo	25 Glad as burning suns that glorious 26 Through the heavenly spaces sway, 27 Haste ye brothers, on your way, 28 Joyous as a knight victorious.
		chorus	Repetition verse 27-28
	fortissimo	orchestra	fugato strumentale
allegro assai	fortissimo	chorus	Repetition verse 1-8
andante maestoso	fortissimo	tenors and basses	29 Love toward countless millions swelling, 30 Wafts one kiss to all the world!
		chorus	Repetition verse 29-30
	forte	tenors and basses	31 Surely, o'er yon stars of heaven, 32 A kind Father has His dwelling!
		chorus	Repetition verse 31-32

PROGRESS	TEMPI	PERFORMERS	LYRICS
adagio ma non troppo ma divoto	piano crescendo sino a fortissimo	chorus	33 Fall ye postrate, O ye millions! 34 Dost thy Maker feel, O World? 35 Seek Him o'er yon **stars** of heaven, 36 O'er the stars rise His pavilions!
	pianissimo	chorus, canon unisono	Repetition verse 36
allegro energico sempre ben marcato	forte	chorus, double fugue sopranos altos tenors basses	Repetition verse 1-4 Repetition verse 29-30 Repetition verse 29-30 Repetition verse 1-4
	piano	orchestra quasi muta (alternating) basses tenors altos sopranos	Repetition verse 33-36 Repetition verse 33-36 Repetition verse 33-36 Repetition verse 33-36
allegro ma non tanto	piano	tenor and baritone soli, soprano and alto, echo soli	Repetition verse 2
		the same, fugal	Repetition verse 5
		soli and chorus	Repetition verse 5-6
		chorus	Repetition verse 7-8
poco adagio	piano in crescendo	chorus	Repetition verse 5-6
		chorus and soli	Repetition verse 7-8
prestissimo	forte	chorus	Repetition verse 29-32 Repetition verse 1-2
	fortissimo	chorus	Repetition verse 1

Beethoven's *Ninth Symphony* (*Choral*), generally considered his masterpiece, forms a synthesis between global philosophical conscience and human existence. The *Ninth Symphony* was the outcome of a long and exhausting creative process. In 1822, the young composer Luigi Schlosser approached Beethoven with a request for commentary on his writing, and the great composer replied as follows:

Often, sometimes even very often, I spend a considerable amount of time on my thoughts, before entrusting them to paper. My memory, however, remains reliable, so once a theme has entered my mind, I can be sure I'll never forget it. I change a lot, reject a lot, or I continue the search, until I'm satisfied; then my mind starts to work on a process in length, width, height and depth. As soon as I know what I want, I can't loose the basic concept anymore.

The text of Schiller's "Ode to Joy," in Beethoven's version, as it is sung in the last movement of the Ninth Symphony. The first recitative is by Beethoven himself. Beethoven was not completely happy with the final result and in the last version he considered doing away with the chorus.

Beethoven began to work on the *Missa Solemnis* in the autumn of 1818. The mass was intended to add luster to the occasion of the inauguration of his friend Archduke Rudolph as Archbishop of Olmütz. This ceremony was to take place on March 9, 1820. Beethoven began the work full of enthusiasm, but had to devote a great deal of time to it, among other things because he searched comprehensively in libraries in order to consult the work of his predecessors (from Palestrina to Mozart). Because no one had commissioned the work and because time was money, Beethoven sought a means of obtaining direct financial profit from his composition. He decided to ask friends and acquaintances for a contribution of 50 ducats per person as "donors." Besides writing to musician friends, composers, publishers and persons of noble blood, he also wrote to Goethe and his musical adviser Zelter. He had apparently forgotten, or deliberately chose to forget, the unfortunate meeting in Teplitz in 1812.

The *Missa Solemnis* was a magnificent synthesis of older musical forms, the well–known liturgical texts, and Beethoven's ideas on progress. The result was an early example of the work of 19th–century composers who managed to combine tradition and innovation in a similar way.

Missa Solemnis, *which Beethoven wrote in 1818 on the occasion of the inauguration of his patron Archduke Rudolf as Bishop of Olmütz in Bohemia. The ceremony took place on March 9, 1820.*

63

The theater of the Karinthian Gate in an etching by Tranquillo Mollo (Vienna, Historisches Museum der Stadt). The famous concert of May 7 1824, in which the Ninth Symphony was premiered and parts of the Missa Solemnis were played, took place here.

Right: The title page of the "40 variations on a theme by Beethoven," dedicated to him and composed by his patron and pupil Archduke Rudolf.

A house concert in the 18th century, a painting of the Neopolitan School (Milan, Castello Sforzesco).

The *Ninth Symphony* and the *Missa Solemnis* were highpoints of innovation in Beethoven's time. But in the practice of music great changes had also taken place during Beethoven's lifetime. Concerts no longer only took place in the great royal courts or in the houses of the rich, and increasingly large halls were used for public concerts. This allowed larger orchestras, which Beethoven's later work demanded.

On the other hand, in his last years Beethoven also occupied himself with works for small groups of musicians, such as the last string quartets. He had already written a good deal of chamber music, the piano trios for example, and his early string quartets (including the *Razumowsky Quartets*). Count Razumowsky had established one of the best string quartets in Austria – friends of Beethoven played in this quartet and the composer wrote music specially for it.

A string quartet, the *String Quartet no. 16, opus* 135, would also be Beethoven's final work.

Beethoven composed a great deal of chamber music. In addition to many string quartets, he also wrote violin and cello sonatas, and piano trios. A number of these trios are light and friendly in character. Beethoven took account of the fact that many dilettantes enjoyed playing them – as can be seen in this Garden Party *(F. Falciatore, Detroit, Institute of Arts).*

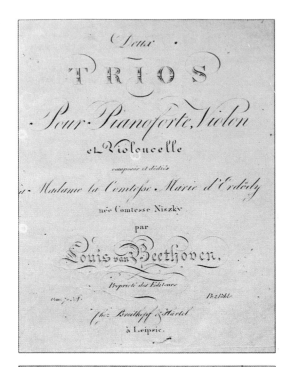

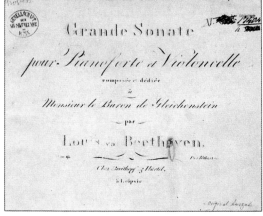

Left: *The title pages of (from top to bottom) the two* Trios *for violin, cello, and piano, opus 70; the* Sonata *for piano and cello, opus 69; and the two* Sonatas *for piano and cello, opus 102.*

Above: *Title page of the* Kreuzer Sonata *for violin and piano, opus 47, dedicated to the violinist of the same name, Rudolphe Kreuzer, a celebrity in his time. According to the title page, the sonata was "written in a very concertante style, almost as a concerto". It is characterized by an intense dialogue between the two instruments which manifest themselves to the same plan, with dynamic and powerful contrasts. In May 1803, in the famous Augarten concert hall in Vienna, Beethoven himself performed the sonata with the violinist Bridgetower.*

The Piano

The piano (in "grand" form) came into being in around 1709 in Florence in the atelier of Bartolomeo Cristofori, and was named a "gravicembalo col piano e forte," later also known as the "Hammerklavier." This was an instrument intended to overcome the limitations of its predecessor, the harpsichord. In order to achieve this, several essential changes were made. The most important was that the strings were no longer plucked by plectra, but struck with hammers covered with felt. Furthermore, for the first time the strings could be made to sound soft (in Italian, "piano") or loud (in Italian, "forte") and – thanks to an ingenious device in the versions which quickly succeeded one another after the "Hammerklavier" – this could be done without the pianist having to release the key. Furthermore, with the aid of pedals, still more effects could be achieved (differences in volume, muting, and resonance). Towards 1770 the grand piano had reached its final form, those built by the Stein company being favorites, also with Mozart.

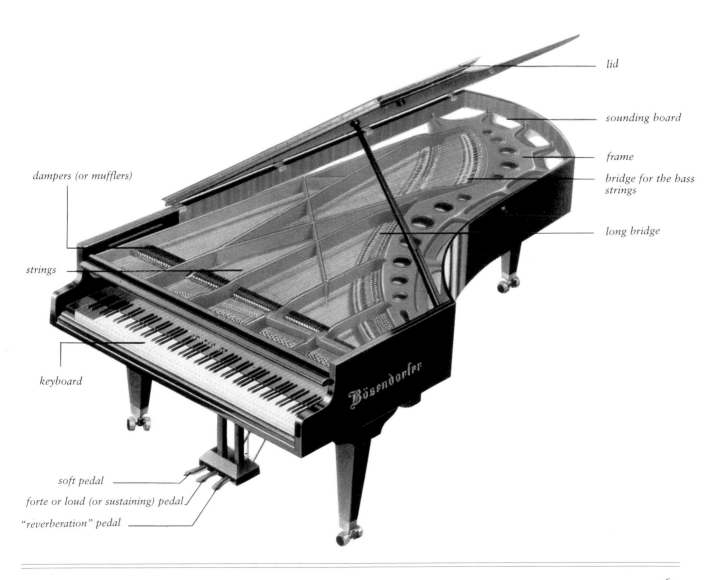

lid

sounding board

frame

bridge for the bass strings

long bridge

dampers (or mufflers)

strings

keyboard

soft pedal

forte or loud (or sustaining) pedal

"reverberation" pedal

The Streicher piano factory in Vienna, where Beethoven often put in an appearance.

Although during the last years of his life Beethoven was a celebrated and successful composer, he could no longer support himself very well and his private life was not particularly pleasant. His nephew Karl, whom he had adopted, was extremely unhappy at boarding school and had also suffered much from his uncle's uncompromising moralism, his total lack of psychological insight, and sense of reality. They had often quarelled and on July 29, 1826, at the age of fifteen, Karl attempted to commit suicide. In a secluded spot he fired several bullets at himself, but remained alive. For Beethoven this was clear and bitter evidence of his own failings as a guardian.

After his suicide attempt, Karl passed into the care of Beethoven's friend, Stephan Breuning. The police considered further inquiries to be unnecessary and Karl was able to join a regiment stationed at Iglau. Beethoven wanted to spend some time with the boy before he had to leave, and they travelled together to the estate of Beethoven's brother, Johann, where they stayed for four months as paying guests. From Beethoven's notebooks we know that during this period he was filled with despair about the approaching separation and the failure of his dream – ideal fatherhood. A quarrel with his brother Johann put an end to their stay and on December 1, 1826 Beethoven returned to Vienna.

The "Schwarzspanierhaus," a former cloister a short distance from the house of the Von Breuning family, and the last place where Beethoven lived.

In October 1825, Beethoven had changed his residence for the umpteenth time. He would spend his last years in what was known as the Schwarzspanierhaus, a former cloister, a short distance from the house of his friends, the Breuning family. One night, after a journey in an open milk cart during a storm, Beethoven returned to this house. When he got home he went straight to bed and sent for the doctor who diagnosed pneumonia. On January 3rd, Karl left to join his regiment and Beethoven remained behind, alone. On top of the pneumonia, he had an attack of jaundice, with dropsy as a complication. In the first weeks of 1827 three operations were necessary, and after that Beethoven never left his bed. He was extremely conscious of his poor prospects, and he was despondent at the absence of his beloved nephew. In the will that he made during these days he named Karl as his sole heir.

Beethoven's financial situation had also deteriorated, and it was only thanks to his friends and, in particular, to the London Philharmonic Society and its director George Smart, that his last months were not too wretched. Old friends and new gathered by his sickbed, and the ten–year–old son of his old friend Stephan Breuning, in particular, provided a source of diversion. Little Gerhard came by every day, concerned himself with Beethoven's welfare, gave him his medicine, brought food from home to him, and lent him his books. Beethoven called him "my Ariel, light as the wind" and enjoyed seeing him.

Right: *Anschelm Hüttenbrenner in a lithograph by Joseph Teltscher (Vienna, Nationalbibliothek). Beethoven died during one of his visits on March 26, 1827.*

Beethoven's death throes began on March 24th and lasted for two days. At the moment of his death – as a remarkable irony of fate – the so detested wife of his brother Johann was standing by his bed, together with a relative stranger, the musician Anselm Hüttenbrenner. Years later, in a letter to Alexander Thayer, one of Beethoven's most important biographers, Hüttenbrenner described Beethoven's last moments as follows: *At five o'clock in the afternoon he was unconscious and embroiled in his death throes when suddenly a flash of lightning accompanied by a peal of thunder illuminated the room in a spectacular manner: on the roofs of the houses, visible through the window, snow fell. After this highly remarkable natural phenomenon, which disconcerted me greatly, Beethoven opened his eyes wide; he raised his right arm, fist clenched, and stared for a few seconds with a proud and menacing gaze into the emptiness before him. When his hand fell back on the bed, his eyes stayed half closed. With my right hand I lifted his head, and I laid my left hand on his breast: he had stopped breathing, and his heart was still.*

Left: *Beethoven's workroom in the "Schwarzspanierhaus." This drawing by Johann Nepomuk Hoechle was made three days after the death of the composer (Vienna, Historisches Museum der Stadt).*

Ludwig van Beethoven on his deathbed.

Vienna, March 28, 1827. The funeral procession leaves the house of Ludwig van Beethoven on its way to the church in Alserstrasse. The procession then proceeded to the churchyard in Währing. As can be clearly seen in this watercolor by Franz Stöber (Bonn, Beethovenhaus), the whole of Vienna turned out for the funeral of the famous deceased. The bier, on the left in the painting, was carried by eight musicians, among them Franz Schubert.

His funeral took place two days later, on March 28, 1827, and according to Beethoven's friend Zmeskall, the ceremony was attended by between twenty and thirty thousand people. The coffin was carried by eight musicians, among whom the composer Franz Schubert, who himself would die a year later, aged thirty-one. The funeral oration was written by Beethoven's friend, the poet Franz Grillparzer, and delivered at the Währing graveyard by the actor Heinrich Anschütz. The last sentence read: *He who comes after him cannot continue on his path but must*

View of the churchyard in Währing, an engraving by Michael Aigner.
At Beethoven's grave the actor Heinrich Anschütz read the funeral address written by Franz Grillparzer (here in a watercolor by Maurice–Michel Daffinger).

begin again, for this forerunner has left off his work at the point where the uttermost bounds of art are to be found.

The Most Important Works of Ludwig van Beethoven

Vocal Works

Fidelio

Choral fantasy, op. 80

Mass in D major, op. 123, "Missa Solemnis"

Symphonies

No. 1 in C major, op. 21

No. 2 in D major, op. 36

No. 3 in E flat major, op. 55, "Eroica"

No. 4 in B flat major, op. 60

No. 5 in C minor, op. 67

No. 6 in F major, op. 68, "Pastoral"

No. 7 in A major, op. 92

No. 8 in F major, op. 93

No. 9 in D minor, op. 125, "Choral"

Piano Sonatas	*No. 8, "Pathétique," op. 13*
	No. 14, "Moonlight," op. 27
	No. 21, "Waldstein," op. 53
	No. 23, "Appassionata," op. 57
	No. 26, "Les Adieux," op. 81a
	No. 29, "Hammerklavier," op. 106
Concertos	*For piano:*
	No. 4 in C minor, op. 37
	No. 4 in G major, op. 58
	No. 5 in E flat major, op. 73, "Emperor"
	Violin concerto in D major, op. 61
	Triple concerto in C major (piano, violin, cello), op. 56
Chamber Music	*Septet in E flat major, op. 20*
	Violin sonata in F major, op. 24, "Frühling"
	Violin sonata in A major, op. 47, "Kreutzer"
	Piano trio in B flat major, op. 97, "Archduke"
	"Razumowsky quartets," op. 59
	Late string quartets, op. 130–135